In the Air

Samantha Berger • Betsey Chessen

Scholastic Inc.
New York • Toronto • London • Auckland • Sydney

Acknowledgments

Literacy Specialist: Linda Cornwell

National Science Consultant: David Larwa

Design: Silver Editions

Photo Research: Amla Sanghvi

Endnotes: Paul Hack

Endnote Illustrations: Craig Spearing

———————————

Photographs: Cover: Paul Brou/The Stock Market; p. 1: Myrleen Ferguson/Photo Edit;
p. 2: Paul Brou/The Stock Market; p. 3: G. Contarokes/The Stock Market;
p. 4: Gary Breitnacher/Tony Stone Images; p. 5: Hubert Camille/Tony Stone Images;
p. 6: David Lawrence/The Stock Market; p. 7: David Fleetham/FPG International; p. 8: Alain
Chambon/Image Bank; p. 9: Philip Wallick/FPG International; pp. 10–11: Visual Horizons/FPG
International; p. 12: Joseph Drivas/Image Bank.

Library of Congress Cataloging-in-Publication Data
Berger, Samantha.
In the air/Samantha Berger, Betsey Chessen.
p.cm. --(Science emergent readers)
Summary: Simple text and photographs introduce such conveyances
as an airplane, hot air balloon, helicopter, blimp, or space shuttle.
ISBN 0-439-08124-6 (pbk.: alk. paper)
1. Airplanes--Juvenile literature. 2. Flying machines--Juvenile literature.
[1. Flying machines. 2. Airplanes.] I. Chessen, Betsey, 1970-. II. Title. III. Series.
TL547.B41775 1999
387.7'3--dc21   98-53311
CIP AC

1   2   3   4   5   6   7   8   9   10   08   03   02   01   00   99

In the air you might see . . .

an airplane,

a seaplane,

or a helicopter.

You might see a parachute,

a parasail,

or a hang glider.

You might see a balloon,

a blimp,

or a biplane . . .

even a space shuttle!

In The Air

Look up in the sky, day or night, and you might see an airplane, a parachute, a hot air balloon, or maybe even a space shuttle blasting into space! These remarkable machines, once thought to be impossible to build, have now become an everyday part of life. They can carry us from place to place, help monitor our weather, and explore our universe. They can even travel faster than your voice can travel across a room!

Airplanes Have you ever wanted to fly? Airplanes are used to fly people and things all over the world and are the fastest form of transportation. Though there are many different types of planes, they all use wings to soar upon the air, engines to achieve great speed, and navigational instruments to allow them to fly at night and through bad weather.

Seaplanes Airplanes that have wheels need large areas of flat land, or a runway, in order to safely take off and land. Seaplanes have special attachments called floats so they can take off and land on water. Some airplanes, called amphibians, have both wheels and floats, and they can take off and land on either land or water.

Helicopters Helicopters are flying machines that use spinning wings, or blades, to gain lift straight up off the ground. They can fly in all directions, even backward, and can hover in one position just above the ground. They are often used in rescue missions and to transport people to and from mountains, where an ordinary airplane could not possibly land.

Parachutes and parasails If you ever jump out of a plane, don't forget your parachute! Parachutes catch the air much like a tree leaf that falls slowly to the ground. Some parachutes allow you to steer so you can land in a safe place. A parasail is a parachute that is attached to a boat by a very long cable. The boat tows you along, and as it picks up speed, the parasail catches the wind and rises above the water.

Hang gliders If you have ever wanted to soar like an eagle, hang gliding is the sport for you. Attached to a pair of wings, you can run off a cliff or hilltop and fly above the surface of the earth. You will get a real bird's-eye view, as you will be looking straight down to the ground below.

Hot air balloons Hot air balloons were the first real flying machines. Since hot air is lighter than cold air, filling a balloon with hot air and attaching it to a basket can actually lift you off the ground. People took great interest in ballooning as soon as it was invented, and it remains a popular sport today. Crowds from all over world gather to watch hundreds of colorful balloons lift off at once—a spectacular sight for those of us still on the ground. Unmanned balloons carry instruments that report information about weather conditions.

Blimps If you've ever been to an outdoor sports arena, you may have seen one of these enormous airships floating overhead. Blimps are filled with helium gas, allowing them to float like a carnival balloon. In the early 1900s they were used to make long trips across the Atlantic Ocean. Back then they were filled with hydrogen, a flammable gas, and many disasters occurred due to fire.

Biplanes Biplanes are double-winged planes that were developed just before World War I. They were easier to fly than single-winged planes because the extra set of wings helped to keep them steady in the air, which was important in mid-air battles with enemy planes. Today you might see one at an air show doing loops and other acrobatics in the air.

Space shuttle Perhaps the most spectacular takeoff you could see is the launching of a space shuttle. The shuttle has three jet engines of its own and is attached to two booster rockets and a large fuel tank. The shuttle is rocketed into the sky, but by the time it reaches space the rockets and fuel tank have detached. The shuttle can then return to the earth using its own engines to reenter the atmosphere and glide to a safe landing.